THE
LEADERSHIP POCKETBOOK

2nd Edition
Fiona Elsa Dent

Drawings by Phil Hailstone

"A pragmatic and practical guide that is as helpful to those new to leadership as it is in reminding seasoned leaders how to make sense of leadership in a complex world. Fiona has distilled her huge experience into an accessible pocketbook - it's this that makes this different."
Marcus Powell, Director, Leadership & Organisational Development, The King's Fund

"Understanding the juggernaut that is leadership can be a real challenge for most. This book beautifully navigates the context and behaviours of leadership while offering some simple self-awareness techniques to help you develop your own authentic leadership style."
Dr Kerrie Fleming, Director, Ashridge Leadership Centre

Published by:
Management Pocketbooks Ltd
Laurel House, Station Approach, Alresford, Hants SO24 9JH, U.K.
Tel: +44 (0)1962 735573   Fax: +44 (0)1962 733637
Email: sales@pocketbook.co.uk
Website: www.pocketbook.co.uk

First edition published 2003. ISBN 978 1 903776 10 0

This revised edition published 2012. Reprinted 2014, 2016. ISBN 978 1 906610 46 3

E-book ISBN 978 1 908284 28 0

British Library Cataloguing-in-Publication Data – A catalogue record for this book is available from the British Library.

Design, typesetting and graphics by **efex ltd** Printed in U.K.

CONTENTS

WHO THIS BOOK IS FOR

This book is for **YOU** if you accept that **leaders are not born into leadership. They can and do grow and develop!**

Leaders exist in all walks of life and at all levels in organisations. Some of today's best known leaders were not born into great families destined for leadership positions: Richard Branson of Virgin, Oprah Winfrey, Media Proprieter and Angela Merkel, German Chancellor, grew into their roles. They have all faced challenges, change, ups and downs, and have persisted to develop and create their own particular brand of leadership. They all have certain qualities in common but, equally, they are very different people.

As a leader in any situation you need to understand the basic principles of leadership, the role of the leader, the skills typical of the effective leader and some of the challenges facing leaders in today's business environment. However, perhaps the most necessary skill for any leader is self-awareness - to know about yourself, to realise what your leadership strengths and weaknesses are and in what directions you must continue to develop.

It is generally accepted that in current society and organisational life leadership is not simply reserved for those in assigned leadership positions. Frequently we experience amazing evidence of *good* leadership in surprising people and places, suggesting that leadership is often contextual or situational. All individuals should be aware of their skills, abilities and knowledge and take leadership opportunities when they arise.

THE NATURE OF LEADERSHIP

THE NATURE OF LEADERSHIP

DEFINITIONS

'Leadership is a potent combination of strategy and character, but if you must be without one be without strategy.' **Norman Schwarzkopf**

'Leadership is not just about producing the right numbers. Leadership is about setting the right tone in the organisation. It's about ethos, it's about what you stand for, it's about trust.' **Sir Stuart Rose**

'Before you are a leader, success is all about growing yourself. When you become a leader it is all about growing others.' **Jack Welch**

'Leaders are put into the position of making judgements on the behalf of others.' **Jonathan Gosling - Director, Exeter Centre For Leadership**

'Innovation distinguishes between a leader and a follower.' **Steve Jobs**

'Effective leadership is not about making speeches or being liked; leadership is defined by results not attributes.' **Peter F Drucker**

'As we look into the next century leaders will be those who empower others.' **Bill Gates**

THE NATURE OF LEADERSHIP

MY DEFINITION OF A LEADER

- 'Someone who inspires me, takes an interest in me as a person and who works with me and others to achieve a commonly shared vision or goal.'

- What is your definition?

_____

_____

_____

_____

_____

_____

LEADERSHIP - SOME OF THE THEORIES

There have been many theories, approaches and ideas about leadership which have been written about over the years - here are some of the most common ones:

- **'Leaders are born not made'** – an old fashioned ideal, largely borne out of the historical perspective of being born to lead by right of birth

- **Situational Leadership** – Ken Blanchard and Paul Hersey's theory that one's leadership style varies according to the situation and that the necessary skills can be developed

- **Charismatic Leadership** – focuses on traits, qualities and personality. While charisma is often regarded as a key quality necessary to be an effective leader, alone it is not enough

- **Transactional Leadership** – similar in nature to the role of the manager. Leaders have a very clear idea of their goals and objectives, which they communicate to their followers and then motivate them to achieve the targets

- **Transformational Leadership** – this type of leadership focuses on the relationship between the leader and the followers. Typically, leaders who use this style have a strong self-awareness and use a range of *soft* skills to gain commitment from others

- **Behavioural Leadership** – is all about what the leader does and how they are perceived to do it; in other words, the behaviours they use in day-to-day life

- **Authentic Leadership** – where the leader is true to themselves and relates to others in a consistent and genuine way

- **Leaders in Society** – recognising that business leaders play a leadership role in wider society as well as in their organisations

THE NATURE OF LEADERSHIP

LEADERSHIP TODAY

The eight approaches summarised are just some of the more common leadership theories that have gained popularity in recent decades. Of the eight, those focusing on behaviours, skills and attitudes that can be developed are the most favoured today, namely:

- Situational
- Transformational
- Behavioural
- Authentic

In other words, to be a leader you must be able to recognise what's required for the situation and for the people involved and be able to adapt your behaviour accordingly, all in a genuine and authentic way. In addition, there is growing interest and support in seeing business leaders as leaders in society.

THE NATURE OF LEADERSHIP

LEADERS AND POWER

Anyone who is a leader or takes on a leadership position takes on a position of power. But what is power? The Oxford Dictionary of Current English (2001) defines it as: *the ability to do or act* and *influence/authority*. So what does this mean for the leader?

We all have many sources of power:
- Position or role - in the organisation
- Control of, or access to, resources
- Relationship or network - accessibility to relevant others

- Information - ability to access it
- Personality - our own
- Skills or knowledge

The important issue about power is not so much the source of our power but rather how we use it.

LEADERS AND POWER

How you use or misuse power is absolutely your own choice. We've all heard the saying, *the power has gone to his/her head*, and no doubt we can all think of people who fit this description. The important thing is to ensure it is never used to describe you.

Consider your own sources of power and how you use them.

Exercise: think of someone you have known who has misused their power, note down who it was, what they did and how it made you feel:

_____

_____

_____

_____

_____

LEADERSHIP - ASSIGNED OR EMERGENT

When a person is appointed to a leadership position this is an *assigned* leadership role. However, on occasions some people can and do emerge from a group to take on a leadership role. Often these *emergent leaders* are people who have specific skills to suit a particular situation.

For instance, in my role as a management trainer I often work with groups in the outdoors. It never ceases to surprise me when the least likely person takes on the role of the leader in some of the more puzzling exercises. In these situations often a quieter member of the group comes to the fore and leads the team to success.

Have you ever unexpectedly found yourself in the role of a leader? Reflect on when, why and what you did including the skills you used.

LEVELS OF LEADERSHIP

Leaders exist at all levels in an organisation and it is worth reflecting on which particular level you are at. Don't dismiss what you do because you think you are not *senior* enough.

Look at the definitions on the following page and mark onto the chart the level of your own role.

STRATEGIC LEADER

OPERATIONAL LEADER

TEAM LEADER

LEVELS OF LEADERSHIP - DEFINITIONS

- **Strategic Leader** - a leader at the top level of the organisation who has responsibility for a range of organisational functions, the people in these functions and for contributing to major decisions.

- **Operational Leader** - a leader in the organisation who has responsibility for a departmental function, all the people in that function and for contributing to decisions in their own specialist area.

- **Team Leader** - a leader who operates at team level whose prime responsibility is for the people who work with them and the achievement of the tasks for which they are jointly responsible.

Each of these levels of leadership requires similar and some different skills and competences. In each case the definition of the skill or competence may vary slightly to take account of the particular needs of the role, its level and the environment within which it operates. On pages 34 to 38 there are short questionnaires examining these competences and your skill level.

(15)

'Leadership and learning are indispensable to each other.'
John F Kennedy

THE LEADER IN TODAY'S BUSINESS ENVIRONMENT

THE BUSINESS ENVIRONMENT

Sustainability

Need for Corporate Responsibility

Globalisation

THE ORGANISATION

Focus on the Customer

Flatter Organisations

Empowerment

Mergers

Pressures for Improved Quality of Life

More work in Teams

THE LEADER

Delayering

Cross-functional Working

Increased Workload
Survive Uncertainty
Multi-Skilled
Continuous Development

Job Losses

Effects of Technology

Environmental Pressures

Out-sourcing

Focus on Quality and Profitability

Climate Change

Take-overs

Increased Link between Pay and Performance

Uncertainty

W.W.W

Increased competition

Rise of Emerging Markets

Complexity

MODEL

LEADERSHIP AND CHANGE

We live in turbulent times, the world is changing rapidly, technological advances alone have a significant effect on all of our lives on a daily basis. Leaders in all walks of life are affected by many of these factors and by other changes shown on the model.

The business environment facing most of us today is vastly different from the world that faced many of the oft quoted famous leaders of previous generations. Leaders today must be more self-aware, agile and open to learning than many of their historical counterparts.

We need leaders at all levels of organisational life. People who will inspire others, take responsibility and get things done. Throughout my life I have been pleasantly surprised by the people who emerge as leaders and the circumstances in which they emerge, such as:

- When organising a social event at work
- When a special task needs doing
- When taking part in sports
- In a crisis

THE LEADER IN TODAY'S BUSINESS ENVIRONMENT

LEADER OR MANAGER?

Are all managers leaders? The single fact of being put in charge of others does not immediately confer leadership status.

Organisations need both managers and leaders - sometimes they are one and the same. However, many managers will never make the grade as leader and many leaders are hopeless managers. Both leaders and managers have their role to play in business life today but the two roles are not one and the same.

For me the significant difference between a leader and a manager is that:

- A **manager** will be appointed to a position and has the possibility of developing leadership skills and of being recognised as a leader, whereas.....

- A **leader** is recognised by the people around them as someone who provides leadership for them in a particular situation whatever the individual's official role

Think of people who have impressed you as effective leaders. What made them special?

WHICH LEADERS HAVE NOT IMPRESSED YOU?

I guess we've all also come across poor leaders - people who've taught us what **not** to do!

In my case, my first experience of a bad leader was in a job where I experienced a team leader who was highly controlling, who never wanted to try out anything new, who always wanted things done his way and who never listened to me or the others in the team.

Can you think of someone (perhaps more than one) who has had a negative effect on you and consequently illustrated how **not** to lead?

In my case this man was simply a manager and not a very good one at that!

A MODEL FOR LEADERSHIP

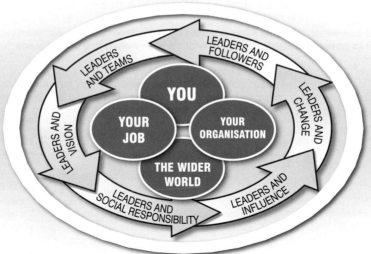

A MODEL FOR LEADERSHIP

The model illustrates the key aspects of the role that an individual has to consider in order to be effective. The overlapping circles in the inner core represent:

YOU – your personality, your values, your beliefs, your behaviour all play a role in how you conduct yourself as a leader.

YOUR JOB – the role that you have at work and when you lead.

YOUR ORGANISATION – also affects the way you lead. The type of organisation, the industry sector it is in and the typical way things are done in the organisation are significant.

THE WIDER WORLD – what's going on in the broader social context, and what that means for your role as a leader.

These four areas are covered in the next two sections: *Key skills and competences* and *Leadership and YOU*.

THE LEADER IN TODAY'S BUSINESS ENVIRONMENT

A MODEL FOR LEADERSHIP

The six arrows surrounding the inner core detail and represent major considerations for leaders in today's society:

The role teams play in the leader's life.

Being able to inspire others about your plans and ideas.

Creating value by benefiting your business and wider society at the same time.

LEADERS AND TEAMS

LEADERS AND FOLLOWERS

LEADERS AND CHANGE

LEADERS AND VISION

LEADERS AND SOCIAL RESPONSIBILITY

LEADERS AND INFLUENCE

The importance of all the people around you.

A reality for all of us today but what role does the leader play?

A key leadership competence used daily.

These areas are all dealt with in different sections of this pocketbook. There are thoughts, ideas and exercises to stimulate your mind and help you to think about your own perspectives on these issues in your leadership role.

KEY SKILLS AND COMPETENCES

KEY SKILLS AND COMPETENCES

A PERFECT LEADER?

All leaders require a broad range of skills, competences and qualities. Some of these are common to all leaders and some – those that depend on the particular situation, leadership level and personality of the individual concerned – are not.

There is no one definitive list to describe the perfect leader. However, in my recent research on leadership I have read many of the major texts on the subject written by the key thinkers in this area. While there is no completely common list of these necessary qualities, there certainly seems to be a lot of consensus on some of the general themes.

The key themes appear to be:

- Self-confidence
- Self-awareness
- Trustworthiness
- Visionary
- Adaptability
- Change agent
- Systems thinker

- Credibility
- Sociable communicator
- Decision-maker
- Analytical
- Political awareness
- Socially responsible
- Literate on global issues

- Energy
- Empathy
- Open-minded
- Strategic
- People-focused
- Authentic

KEY SKILLS AND COMPETENCES

WHAT YOUR ORGANISATION NEEDS

Before we move on to a range of questionnaires that will help you reflect on and review your own range of leadership skills, qualities and competences, I suggest you consider what's actually important for your own situation and in your own organisation.

Questions to help you reflect:

- What sector of business are you in: service, industry or manufacturing?
- Is yours a growing, unstable or shrinking organisation?
- Predominantly national or international?
- Hierarchical or fairly flat?
- What's happening in general in your industry?
- How long has your current CEO/Chairman/most senior person been in situ?
- How clear are the organisation's strategic and business plans?
- How well communicated are they?
- How adaptable to change is your organisation?
- How long have you been with the organisation?
- How long have you been in your current role?

KEY SKILLS AND COMPETENCES

WHAT YOUR ORGANISATION NEEDS

Now reflect on your thoughts and, perhaps, take the opportunity to make notes:

- What's happening in the wider world that will have an impact on your organisation?
- What's happening in your organisation at the moment?
- What are the current ideas on the strategic and business plans for the future?
- What is happening in your particular part of the organisation?
- What leadership skills, competences and qualities do you think will be necessary now and in the future?

KEY SKILLS AND COMPETENCES

'Self-awareness is central
to being a successful leader. '
Kouzes & Posner
in *The Future of Leadership*,
2001

KEY SKILLS AND COMPETENCES

RAISING YOUR AWARENESS

Over the next few pages are a set of questionnaires to help you reflect on and assess your own range of leadership skills, competences and qualities.

The first questionnaire examines some general areas which I believe to be important for any leader at any level in an organisation. The three questionnaires that follow from that are linked to the three levels of leadership:

- Strategic
- Operational
- Team

You should focus in the first instance on the one which is the most appropriate for you in your current role and then move on to the one that you are aspiring to in your next career move.

Fully answer each questionnaire, then complete the reflection and analysis sections that follow, as this will help you to synthesise and make sense of the data.

KEY SKILLS AND COMPETENCES

LEADERSHIP QUESTIONNAIRES

INSTRUCTIONS AND GUIDANCE

The four questionnaires that follow list various criteria which appear to be relevant for effective and successful leadership today. The first questionnaire applies to all levels of leadership. The others are appropriate for different types of leaders and tend to relate to your leadership level in the organisation. Select the one most relevant to your position The three leadership level questionnaires also include suggestions about other Pocketbooks that may help you to develop your knowledge and skills.

Instructions
Read the questions and circle the level of skill or competence which you believe best describes you.

1 = not skilled/no ability in this area   4 = good skill/ability in this area
2 = some skill/ability in this area   5 = highly skilled/high ability in this area
3 = skilled/able in this area

You may also like to ask others who experience your leadership how they would rate you. If you choose to ask others for feedback remember to select people you trust to give fair feedback and who will be willing to discuss this with you. **Health warning! Remember, if you decide to do this you may hear some things you wish you hadn't!**

LEADERSHIP QUESTIONNAIRE

COMMON ATTRIBUTES, SKILLS AND COMPETENCES

Credibility – has sound reputation and track-record ▢1 ▢2 ▢3 ▢4 ▢5

Decisiveness – makes decisions and follows through to outcome ▢1 ▢2 ▢3 ▢4 ▢5

Integrity – demonstrates honesty and fairness ▢1 ▢2 ▢3 ▢4 ▢5

Self-confidence – demonstrates self-belief ▢1 ▢2 ▢3 ▢4 ▢5

Energy – has ability and capacity to work hard ▢1 ▢2 ▢3 ▢4 ▢5

Self-awareness – understands own character, personality and motives ▢1 ▢2 ▢3 ▢4 ▢5

Adaptability – maintains effectiveness in change situations ▢1 ▢2 ▢3 ▢4 ▢5

Listening – demonstrates good understanding by questioning and clarifying ▢1 ▢2 ▢3 ▢4 ▢5

Tenacity – sticks with challenges until settled ▢1 ▢2 ▢3 ▢4 ▢5

Persuasiveness – has ability to convince others ▢1 ▢2 ▢3 ▢4 ▢5

Empathy – shows ability to identify with others inside and outside the organisation ▢1 ▢2 ▢3 ▢4 ▢5

Relationship management – recognises importance of building and developing relationships ▢1 ▢2 ▢3 ▢4 ▢5

Open-mindedness – is accessible to new ideas ▢1 ▢2 ▢3 ▢4 ▢5

Initiative – sees and acts on opportunities ▢1 ▢2 ▢3 ▢4 ▢5

Ambition – has a high need to achieve ▢1 ▢2 ▢3 ▢4 ▢5

Flexibility – able to modify style to suit situation ▢1 ▢2 ▢3 ▢4 ▢5

Trustworthiness – is reliable ▢1 ▢2 ▢3 ▢4 ▢5

Interpersonally aware – uses a range of skills to interact effectively with others ▢1 ▢2 ▢3 ▢4 ▢5

Commitment – shows belief in self and organisation ▢1 ▢2 ▢3 ▢4 ▢5

Authenticity – relates to others in a consistent and genuine way ▢1 ▢2 ▢3 ▢4 ▢5

Globally aware – is literate on global issues and business implications ▢1 ▢2 ▢3 ▢4 ▢5

KEY SKILLS AND COMPETENCES

LEADERSHIP QUESTIONNAIRE

REFLECTION AND ANALYSIS

- What are my top three leadership strengths?

  1. _____ 2. _____ 3. _____

- What are my three weakest areas?

  1. _____ 2. _____ 3. _____

- What does this tell me about my general leadership development needs?

  _____

  _____

  _____

- What steps should I take to begin developing?

  _____

QUESTIONNAIRE: STRATEGIC LEADER

Competence	Skill Level	Relevant Pocketbooks
Leadership – works with others to create right environment for high performance	1 2 3 4 5	Performance Management
Influencing – influences others to make things happen	1 2 3 4 5	Influencing, Negotiator's, Working Relationships, Impact & Presence
Decision-making – makes well-reasoned and thought-through decisions	1 2 3 4 5	Creative Manager's, Decision-making
Interpersonal skills – uses range of skills and approaches to interact effectively with others	1 2 3 4 5	Communicator's, Manager's, Managing Upwards, Meetings, People Manager's, Teamworking
People development – encourages others to develop to their full potential	1 2 3 4 5	Coaching, Developing People, Facilitator's, Learner's, Mentoring, Self-managed Development

Cont'd

KEY SKILLS AND COMPETENCES

QUESTIONNAIRE: STRATEGIC LEADER

Competence	Skill Level	Relevant Pocketbooks
Leading change – adopts proactive approach to change	☐☐☐☐☐	Managing Change
Results focus – delivers results which achieve business objectives	☐☐☐☐☐	Improving Efficiency, Strategy
Strategic thinker – develops long-term business plans to enable strategies to be met	☐☐☐☐☐	Business Planning, Thinker's
Manages resources – uses resources effectively to ensure objectives are met	☐☐☐☐☐	Improving Profitability, Improving Efficiency
Forward planner – defines priorities and plans all resources to achieve business and strategic objectives	☐☐☐☐☐	Personal Success, Time Management
Globally aware – understands the major societal and environmental forces shaping our world and the implications for business	☐☐☐☐☐	

QUESTIONNAIRE: OPERATIONAL LEADER

Competence	Skill Level	Relevant Pocketbooks
Leadership – creates working environment where people are highly motivated and developed	☐ ☐ ☐ ☐ ☐	Motivation
Influencing – has ability to affect others' attitudes, beliefs and behaviours without using force or formal authority	☐ ☐ ☐ ☐ ☐	Influencing, Negotiator's
People management – works with others to get the best from them	☐ ☐ ☐ ☐ ☐	Manager's, People Manager's, Performance Management, Starting In Management, Teamworking
People development – encourages people development by investing own time and effort	☐ ☐ ☐ ☐ ☐	Coaching, Developing People, Facilitator's, Induction, Self-managed Development
Self-management – shows awareness of the skills and processes necessary for effective self-management	☐ ☐ ☐ ☐ ☐	Emotional Intelligence, Personal Success, Time Management, Positive Mental Attitude
Interpersonal skills – uses a range of skills and approaches to interact effectively with others	☐ ☐ ☐ ☐ ☐	Communicator's, Meetings, Networking
Change agent – demonstrates an open mind and copes well with uncertainty and ambiguity	☐ ☐ ☐ ☐ ☐	Managing Change
Decision-making – gathers data in order to evaluate the situation and make effective decisions	☐ ☐ ☐ ☐ ☐	Creative Manager's, Decision-making, Thinker's
Business orientation – shows understanding of how the business works and the marketplace in which it operates	☐ ☐ ☐ ☐ ☐	Balance Sheet, Business Planning, Managing Budgets, Managing Cashflow, Marketing
Socially responsible – champions the need for people to do the right thing for wider society	☐ ☐ ☐ ☐ ☐	

KEY SKILLS AND COMPETENCES

QUESTIONNAIRE: TEAM LEADER

Competence	Skill Level	Relevant Pocketbooks
Leadership – leads team to ensure they are effective, motivated and developed	1 2 3 4 5	Motivation
Teamworker – encourages team members to develop a team spirit	1 2 3 4 5	Empowerment, Teamworking
People management – works with others to got the best from them	1 2 3 4 5	Appraisals, Manager's, People Manager's, Performance Management
People development – uses range of skills and techniques to ensure people have the skill and competence to perform their job	1 2 3 4 5	Coaching, Developing People, Facilitator's, Induction, Learner's, Mentoring, Self-managed Development
Self-management – shows awareness of the skills and approaches necessary for effective self-management	1 2 3 4 5	Personal Success, Positive Mental Attitude, Time Management, Emotional Intelligence
Interpersonal skills – uses range of skills and abilities to interact effectively with others	1 2 3 4 5	Assertiveness, Influencing, Meetings, Networking
Communication – communicates ideas and information clearly and concisely	1 2 3 4 5	Business Presenter's, Writing Skills, Communicator's, Storytelling
Business awareness – demonstrates awareness of the organisation's business and objectives	1 2 3 4 5	Balance Sheet, Business Planning, Managing Budgets, Managing Cashflow, Marketing
External perspective – understands how events and trends in the wider world affect their business	1 2 3 4 5	

37

LEADERSHIP QUESTIONNAIRES

ANALYSIS

Having completed one of the three leadership level questionnaires you should analyse the results and compare them with the results from the previous generic questionnaire.

Ask yourself some or all of the following questions and make a note of your responses:

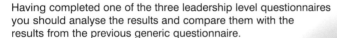

- What are my key skill areas?
- What areas need developing?
- What skills are vital for my current role - what's my skill level in each case?
- What skills help me most as a leader?
- What skills do I need to develop to move to the next level?
- What skills would I like to develop to be even more effective?
- Are there any additional skills I could add?

LEADERSHIP AND YOU

YOUR PERSONAL CODE OF CONDUCT

How you lead will be affected by many things, including:

- Your skills and competences
- Your own experience of being led
- Your organisation's culture
- Your role in the organisation
- Your organisation's attitude to wider society

In addition to the above your own self-concept will have a major impact on how you approach leadership. An individual's self-concept is developed through various social processes and through interaction with others. This self-concept or image determines the behaviour we use in different situations. On a sheet of paper, write down 12 words or phrases that describe you.

LEADERSHIP AND YOU

YOUR PERSONAL CODE OF CONDUCT

Review the 12 words you have used to describe yourself and reflect upon what this says about your own personal values. These values will have a significant effect upon the approach you take as a leader.

A value is defined as *one of the principles you live your life by.* For instance, you may feel that important values for you are to:

● Tell the truth ● Listen and understand others

Think about your life so far and your behaviour as a leader, and try to identify up to six important values you apply to life and leadership:

1 _____ 4 _____

2 _____ 5 _____

3 _____ 6 _____

Now reflect on how this affects the way you approach leading others.

LEADERSHIP AND YOU

LEADERSHIP STYLE

Much is written about leadership style: whether one is more autocratic, democratic, charismatic, collaborative, individualistic, etc. Current and recent research suggests that no one leadership style is best.   However, two key messages do emerge:

● Successful leaders have the ability to vary their style according to the context

● A more participative style seems to be most effective

Personally I believe that real effectiveness depends upon each leader creating and developing their own unique style.

You may like to define your own style or at least have a perspective on your particular preference for leading and working with others. The checklists on the following page encourage you to reflect on a range of words that can be used to describe leadership style. Examine the four lists and tick those words that you believe reflect your own particular style and approach to leadership.

LEADERSHIP STYLE CHECKLISTS

Column 1	Column 2	Column 3	Column 4
☐ Charisma	☐ Encourage	☐ Confident	☐ Sociable
☐ Tell	☐ Facilitate	☐ Intuitive	☐ Co-ordinator
☐ Control	☐ Listen	☐ Visionary	☐ Team-player
☐ Structure	☐ Developer	☐ Networker	☐ Encouraging
☐ Authority	☐ Empower	☐ Persuader	☐ Dependable
☐ Focus	☐ Supportive	☐ Assertive	☐ Sincere
☐ Decision-maker	☐ Self-aware	☐ Change agent	☐ Trustworthy
☐ Responsible	☐ Praise	☐ Results-focussed	☐ Conscientious
☐ Opinionated	☐ Adaptable	☐ Catalyst	☐ Open-minded
☐ Ambitious	☐ Understanding	☐ Convincing	☐ Considerate
☐ TOTAL	☐ TOTAL	☐ TOTAL	☐ TOTAL

Note down the total number of words you have ticked in each column.

LEADERSHIP STYLE REVIEW

The checklists on the previous page examine your preferences in terms of your own particular leadership style.   The words used describe four typical styles:

Directive (Col.1)   – leaders who take control, make decisions and are self-reliant
Coaching (Col.2)   – leaders who focus on developing and involving others
Influencing (Col.3)   – leaders who are confident in their own ability, convincing and drive to achieve
Collaborative (Col.4) – leaders who create harmony and work with and through others

Most of us will have a preference for one style over the other. Your predominant style is the one which has the highest total.

Note down your predominant style   _____

What is your back up style?   _____

What does this tell you about your current approach to leadership? Think about recent leadership situations and the way you dealt with them. Ask yourself:

- Did I get the best out of the situation?   ●   How did the people react to me?
- Were there other approaches which might have been more effective?

LEADERSHIP STYLES COMPARED

ADVANTAGES	DISADVANTAGES
Directive	
- works well in times of crisis	- can appear over-controlling
- good with inexperienced people	- doesn't involve others
- effective when time is an issue	- can stifle creativity
- when you are the most knowledgeable	- ignores the need to motivate others
Coaching	
- develops people	- can be time-consuming
- improves performance	- relies on others to work with them
- raises self-awareness of followers	- assumes people want to develop
- builds trust	
Influencing	
- mobilises people	- may appear manipulative
- can be inspirational	- can be regarded as condescending
- appropriate in times of change	- may appear too pushy
- when you have high credibility	
Collaborative	
- builds consensus and ownership	- relies on others' involvement
- motivates people	- can appear indecisive
- involves others	- relies on others' commitment
- uses others' expertise and experience	- assumes others have knowledge

IMPORTANCE OF ADAPTING STYLE

Understanding your preferred leadership style is important. It also helps you to understand the effect your style has on others and when it is most effective.

However, in today's complex, rapidly changing and multi-faceted business environment it is more important to be able to adapt and vary the style to suit the people involved, the situation you are in and the prevailing business environment.

No one has it all.
It's a matter of fit.
True situational leadership involves calibration of behaviour to fit a given situation.

Adapted from *Relax It's Only Uncertainty*,
Hodgson & White, Prentice Hall, 2001

46

CREATING PERSONAL IMPACT

As a leader, people will be watching you at all times, looking and listening for the messages you convey in your dealings with them.   This means that you have to be very aware of the subtle messages you are conveying to others in what you say and do and how you say and do it. All of this contributes to your personal impact.

Personal impact is all about communication:

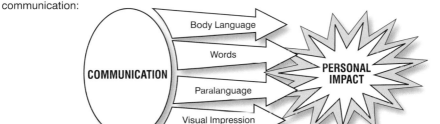

LEADERSHIP AND YOU

CREATING PERSONAL IMPACT

Think about, watch footage of and reflect on some well-known leaders (past and present), for instance:

- Barack Obama
- Christine Lagarde
- Nelson Mandela
- Aung San Suu Kyi
- Bill Clinton
- Tony Blair
- Steve Jobs
- Bill Gates

How would you describe their personal impact?

Now focus on yourself. Consider the impact you typically convey in a variety of interpersonal situations. For instance, think about:

- When you are talking to large groups
- When you are taking part in a meeting
- When you are interacting with one other
- When you meet someone in the car park
- When you walk into a room

Reflect on the messages you are conveying by your visual impression, your body language, the words you use and your paralanguage (how you say things).

How would you describe your personal impact in general? How will this affect your role as a leader?

LEADERSHIP AND YOU

THE 15-SECOND RULE

'When we see someone for the first time, the initial sound/visual "bite" - a combination of their looks, their dress, their bearing and the tenor of their opening remarks - becomes deeply etched in our minds and affects our attitudes to them!'

Michael Shea
in *Personal Impact*

YOUR LEADERSHIP NETWORK

The people you interact with on a regular basis are the people who contribute to your leadership network. To help you understand more about these people it is worth analysing the network you have developed. One way of doing this is to draw a mind map.

You will need a blank sheet of paper and a pencil. Draw a circle in the middle of the sheet and then brainstorm all the people or groups of people by category who form your leadership network. This can get quite detailed, depending upon the number of people you interact with on a regular basis.
Use your own initiative to decide how detailed you wish to be.

Here is a fairly basic sample of a leadership network.

- Other Organisational Contacts
- Boss - John Smith
- Colleagues on Senior Management Team
  - Sonia
  - Rene
  - Imran
  - Jay
  - Mitch
- Direct Reports
  - Sol
  - Julia
  - Ed
  - Cruz
  - Sam
- My Leadership Network
- People in other departments
- My Reports' People
- Customers
- Family and Friends
- Suppliers

LEADERSHIP AND YOU

ANALYSING YOUR LEADERSHIP NETWORK

Having created your leadership network the real meaning comes from the analysis and possibly the annotation of the chart. In order to fully analyse your network you should consider the following questions and, if appropriate, annotate your network map accordingly.

- How would you describe your relationship with each of the people (or groups of people)?

- How important is each person/group of people to your leadership effectiveness?

- What makes each of these people tick?

- What turns them on and off?

- How do you think each of these people regards you as a leader?

SOMEONE TO CONFIDE IN

The role of the leader can be a lonely one. Many people in leadership positions find it difficult to identify an appropriate person/s to share problems or confidential issues with.

This may be one of the contributing factors to the increased usage of the leadership coach. Typically, a leadership coach is an independent individual who provides support, challenge and empathy for the person they are coaching. Finding the right coach for you is, of course, of paramount importance and whoever you choose must be:

- Someone you can trust
- Someone you respect
- Someone you like
- Someone who is empathetic
- Someone you believe can add value to your current performance

You will not always need to establish a formal relationship with a coach. You may be fortunate enough to find someone with all the right qualities from within your own leadership network, for instance:

- Your partner
- A colleague or peer
- Someone in a position similar to your own in a different environment

Whoever you select, remember mutual **trust** and **respect** are vital.

YOUR LEADERSHIP BRAND

You have now looked at a variety of different aspects of your approach to leadership and, no doubt, you are beginning to formulate or articulate your own particular recipe for success in this role - your leadership brand or trademark!

So, how would you define your particular brand of leadership?

What are the key characteristics of your brand?

What do you see as the benefits of your brand?

Can you create an image or slogan to define your leadership brand? (Take a sheet of paper and create a graphic which you feel represents your approach to leadership).

BRAND ME

BRAND ME
AS A LEADER I BELIEVE IN:
- **L** - Loyalty
- **E** - Enthusiasm
- **A** - Awareness of self
- **D** - Drive
- **E** - Empathy
- **R** - Respect

LEADERS AND FOLLOWERS

LEADERS AND FOLLOWERS

LEADERS I KNOW AND MOST ADMIRE

As a leader yourself you have almost certainly worked for or rubbed shoulders with leaders whom you admire. Sometimes it is easy to articulate why you admire them, and sometimes not so easy. It will be useful to reflect upon what it was/is these people do that makes you admire them.

For instance, I remember when my son first started to play football as a child. He was 'led' by a man whose qualities and skills instilled in a group of 8-year olds the importance of learning the skill of football, working as a team to play and, sometimes, to win the game, but above all to enjoy taking part!

I have never forgotten the skills and qualities that man demonstrated to me and the children he coached on a regular basis.

LEADERS I KNOW AND MOST ADMIRE

The skills and qualities my son's football coach demonstrated were:

- Patience (in bucket loads)
- Vision
- Fairness
- Judgement
- Loyalty
- Drive
- Influence
- Passion
- Communication
- Inspiration (even when they were losing - which they did a lot!)
- Respect (for all the kids - his team and the opponents!)

Over the years I have seen many football coaches working with young and impressionable people. Rarely have I seen any demonstrate the skill of this man to inspire and motivate so effectively.

LEADERS WHO HAVE AFFECTED MY LIFE

Reflect back over your life, especially over those times when you have been a follower. Now think about a person who impressed you as an effective leader:

● Who was the person (known to you) that led you most effectively?

_____

● Where and when did you meet them?

_____

● Describe why you have selected this person:

_____

● Make a list of the qualities, skills and attributes this person has that make him or her so special:

_____

LEADERS AND FOLLOWERS

EXPECTATIONS OF THE FOLLOWER

Leaders need followers – without them there would be no need for leaders!

In any organisation followers outnumber leaders. The effectiveness and success of the leaders will, largely, depend upon the relationship that is established between the two parties. It is important that leaders invest time and energy to develop and nurture this relationship.

Followers have certain expectations of the leader and these tend to fall into five main categories:

- **Enthusiasm** – followers want their leader to demonstrate commitment, energy and, above all, inspiration

- **Valued** – followers need to feel that the work they do really matters. They want to feel that their contribution has significance to the bigger picture

- **Appreciated** – we all need to be appreciated and followers want to feel the leader takes a personal interest in them and shows genuine commitment to them

- **Belonging** – as followers we need to feel part of a whole, not simply a cog in a wheel but an important part of a well oiled machine

- **Authenticity** – followers want consistent and genuine leaders

FOLLOWERS RELATING TO YOU

Views on leadership have changed in recent years; gone are the days of the solitary hero. Today it is becoming more important to recognise that those people who work for you or regard you as their leader for some other reason - your followers - should relate to you in a positive sense. The benefits of this positive relationship will usually be seen in the followers':

- Effort
- Morale
- Achievement of goals

Effective leaders today should be approachable and available to their followers. Typical ways of encouraging and enabling your followers to develop a relationship with you include:

- Setting aside *open door* time for people on a regular basis (daily or weekly)
- Walking the talk - or getting out of your office and wandering about and talking to people
- Remembering who people are and what they do
- Communicating relevant information to all concerned on a regular basis
- Celebrating success with your followers and showing appreciation of them
- Recognising when tough messages must be conveyed and communicating them

LEADERS AND FOLLOWERS

BELONGING AND IDENTITY

Followers will tend to perform more effectively if they feel that they belong to a community and, therefore, have a sense of identity with that community.

A sense of belonging and identity is an important element of the authentic leader's role. Followers should be involved in this process.

A sense of belonging and identity is indicated when:

- Teamwork is valued and rewarded
- People are genuinely sensitive and respectful of each others' needs
- You hear the word **we** a lot
- Everyone indicates a common understanding of goals and objectives
- People feel they are valued for who they are by the leader and others
- You hear pride in people's voices when they talk about their work, team, leader
- People enjoy their work and have fun

ENTHUSIASM, ENERGY AND ENGAGEMENT

Engaging your people to work with you is an active part of the leader's role in gaining their followers' respect. You have to earn this. One way of envisaging how this can be earned is to reflect upon your own experience of being a follower. Alternatively, if you were in your followers' shoes, consider what would make you follow you.

In discussing followership with many of my colleagues and programme participants the three E's come up fairly regularly:

- **Enthusiasm** - a genuine interest and eagerness demonstrated
- **Energy** - showing vitality, liveliness and passion
- **Engagement** - the ability to gain and keep a person's attention through communication

Obviously, this is not an exhaustive list but it does summarise three of the most important ingredients a leader requires to inspire others to follow.

Have you got what it takes? Reflect on the things that would make you follow you.

LEADER AS COACH AND MENTOR

There are significant benefits to be gained from taking on the role of coach/mentor, including:
- A sense of achievement in seeing others grow
- Personal satisfaction
- Greater awareness of your followers' skills and abilities
- Relationship building with others
- Demonstration of real interest in others' development - valued and appreciated

Coaching is the process of equipping people to develop themselves. There is no one recipe for success, rather it is a range of techniques which effective leaders adopt:
- Develop trusting relationships with others
- Work with others to identify performance gaps
- Ask specific questions
- Listen to responses
- Give objective and timely feedback
- Identify the right learning opportunity for the person concerned
- Agree targets, goals and review times
- Confirm and appreciate the developed skill/knowledge

LEADER AS COACH AND MENTOR

Reflect on when you have been coached effectively:

- What made it effective?
- What new skills/knowledge did you develop?
- How did you put it into practice?

How can this contribute to your own approach to coaching?

The role of the mentor is slightly different from that of the coach. Typically, a mentor is someone who is willing to share their own personal insights and experiences in order to help another person to develop and grow. Mentors may also play *devil's advocate* by challenging and asking difficult questions (this skill is shared with the coach) to help the mentee to formulate their own ideas.

Can you identify people who have mentored you throughout your career?

Coaching and mentoring are important roles for today's leaders to take on. They can provide leaders with development opportunities, they certainly help in developing relationships with your followers and, almost always, add to your leadership credibility.

LEADERS AND TEAMS

THE ROLE OF THE LEADER IN THE TEAM

Success as a team leader depends on:

- Recognising that you have to vary your style to suit the people in the team and the task faced at the time

- Understanding the variety of stages in a team's development and that each stage demands a different approach (see page 51 in *The Teamworking Pocketbook* for more on this)

- Being prepared to meet your three main challenges:
  - lead the team: as a team which has grown and developed together
  - lead each individual: knowing each individual and their respective strengths and weaknesses, likes and dislikes
  - get the job done: developing, agreeing and setting objectives and goals for individuals and the team to meet

Take a few minutes now to reflect on teams that you have led. What made them special/memorable/effective? What was your role in this?

LEADING DIFFERENT TEAM TYPES

There are many different
types of team, eg:

- Functional Teams
- Cross-functional Teams
- Project Teams
- Virtual Teams
- Remote Teams
- Multi-cultural Teams

Each of these team types has its own
particular characteristics and challenges
which are described on the following pages.

Reflect upon the different teams you
operate in and try to categorise them.
Think about teams that you lead and
teams to which you belong.

TEAM TYPES

TEAM TYPE	CHARACTERISTICS	CHALLENGES
Functional Team	The most frequent type, where the team works together on a daily basis – often a department team	<ul><li>The leader must be present</li><li>Select the right approach for the team, each individual and the task</li><li>Demonstrate real knowledge about each individual</li></ul>
Cross-functional Team	A team that comes together for specific reasons – often a board of directors or senior managers	<ul><li>As the leader is often the first among equals, the main challenge is to adopt the correct approach</li></ul>
Project Team	Set up for a specific purpose/time to undertake a particular task and then disbanded	<ul><li>Gain commitment to the goal and maintain motivation and morale</li><li>Ensure people are appropriately organised</li><li>Keep things on schedule</li><li>Achieve the goal</li></ul>

TEAM TYPES

TEAM TYPE	CHARACTERISTICS	CHALLENGES
Virtual Team	Teams who rarely meet face-to-face but meet using technology – video conferencing/e-mail. Often, people in similar roles but different locations	<ul><li>Establish your credibility</li><li>Manage the emotional element</li><li>Get to know the different people</li><li>Many of these teams start their life with a team-building event to assist in the above</li></ul>
Remote Team	Teams where the leader and the team are based in different locations – eg: sales teams	<ul><li>Ensure sufficient time is spent with each team member</li><li>Provide opportunities for regular contact</li></ul>
Multi-cultural Team	A team of people from different cultural backgrounds – possibly following mergers or takeovers or people working in an international context	<ul><li>Owing to the diversity, the main challenge is to get to know and understand each other</li><li>Be aware of the cultural differences</li></ul>

DEVELOPING THE TEAM: TEAM DYNAMICS

Developing your team involves understanding the dynamics of effective teamworking and effective team behaviour.

- Know the goals and aims of the team

- Know how the *unofficial* leadership processes operate

- Understand how each team member is influenced

- Understand each team member's role - both official (secretary, time-keeper, scribe, etc) and unofficial (joker, devil's advocate, rebel, etc)

- Establish a process for dealing with conflict

- Have an agreed process for problem-solving and decision-making

- Define and agree acceptable and unacceptable behaviour appropriate for each team (this will differ from team to team)

LEADERS AND TEAMS

'The key to success is preparation. I want to be part of the best team in the world. What you say to people on the pitch is not as important as everything you do before you get onto it. The image is made before the game.'

Will Carling
(Rugby Player)

BUILDING HIGH-PERFORMANCE TEAMS

As a leader one always wishes to build a high-performance team - but what does this mean? All teams are different and will operate in different ways and have their own personality. There are, however, certain characteristics which I believe contribute to high-performing teams:

- Demonstrate a keenness to succeed
- Are motivated by their goal
- Members show commitment to each other, the leader and the goal
- Set and achieve challenging targets
- Review targets and goals regularly
- Members show respect for each other
- Members are open and honest in their relationships with each other
- Celebrate success
- Learn and move on from failure or mistakes - no blame culture!
- Get satisfaction from what they are doing and even have **fun**

Think about teams you lead or work in. Look at the list above and tick the characteristics you believe to exist in them? What does this tell you about your teams or team leadership?

LEADERS AND VISION

LEADERS AND VISION

WHAT IS VISION?

The Oxford Dictionary of Current English defines vision as *imaginative insight or statesmanlike foresight*. What does this actually mean in the context of your role as a leader? Frequently, vision is listed as one of the qualities that effective and successful leaders demonstrate.

I believe vision is about generating ideas about the way ahead and, more importantly, being able to articulate these ideas to others in such a way that they can buy-in and understand what you are trying to achieve.

Vision is not about how you are going to do it but about the actual outcome you desire. A vision is a simple yet, possibly, inspirational statement about the way ahead.

A good leader should be able clearly and simply to share the vision they have for their project, department, business unit or organisation.

Can you think of your vision for any current project you are working on? How would you convey it to others?

CREATING THE VISION

A vision is usually created from your own dreams or ideas about the way ahead for a project you are working on, or for your department, division, business unit or, even, organisation. Not only does vision provide direction but it can also provide an enduring sense of purpose and a continued sense of motivation both for yourself and for others. It is about creating and managing change - it can provide meaning in this turbulent world we live in.

Creating the vision involves:
- Having absolute conviction about the issue/project/department/organisation/etc...
- Reflecting upon an outcome/future you really desire
- Questioning what it will look like
- Questioning what it will feel like
- Considering how you will describe it
- Testing your initial ideas out on trusted others
- Building your shared vision with your team
- Involving others in developing the vision to ensure their commitment
- Listen - Ask - Share - Develop

'A vision gives meaning and purpose to your actions. It is the picture on the jigsaw box of life.'

Anon

LEADERS AND VISION

ARTICULATING YOUR VISION

Articulating your vision involves aligning your/your organisation's values, and any thoughts you have on strategy, with the vision.

Articulation, by definition, means that you begin to share your vision with others. This process of sharing will help you to craft your vision into a process that can be communicated more widely to others.

This will help you to:

● Clearly state your own or your organisation's values

● See your route map for the future

● Begin to identify the actionable steps leading to achievement of your vision

COMMUNICATING THE VISION

Communicating your vision involves:
- More than one delivery method
- Passion
- Having the courage of your conviction
- Self-belief/confidence
- Belief that your vision (or dream) could become reality

> 'A leader shapes and shares a vision, which gives point to the work of others.'
> **Charles Handy**

To communicate your vision you could:
- Present your ideas to others – using words and images
- Live your vision – taking every opportunity to discuss, share and articulate it to others
- Use symbolism – ensure everything around you suggests your vision

Some examples of people who have demonstrated good visionary leadership are:

Richard Branson – Virgin   Anita Roddick – Bodyshop
Steve Jobs – Apple   Nelson Mandela – ex-President of South Africa

Can you think of any examples of visionary leaders from your own life?

INSPIRING OTHERS

Defining, developing, articulating and communicating your vision is the easy part; inspiring others to buy into and follow your vision is the real challenge.

Vision is really all about seeing the way ahead, having an imagination, knowing where you are going.

In order to inspire others to follow you in this dream you must be:

- Trusted
- Passionate
- Believable
- Genuine

And your vision must be:

- Simple
- Clear
- Relevant

LEADERS AND INFLUENCE

INFLUENCING AS A PROCESS

To influence effectively and successfully you must do more than simply get your facts together then put them forward in a logical and rational case to the appropriate people.

Influencing is a complex and long-term process which involves:

- Developing relationships with relevant others
- Establishing and maintaining your own credibility
- Gaining the trust of others
- Having patience
- Preparing a well researched case
- Having a good knowledge and understanding of the issue, the stakeholders and the environment, although not necessarily being the expert

Influencing is an emotional process as well as a rational one. You might like to reflect on some recent influencing situations you have found yourself in and focus on the emotions you felt and those displayed by the others involved.

Failure to prepare and plan for influencing situations is often cited by individuals as the most common reason for failure or lack of success.

LEADERS AND INFLUENCE

THE INFLUENCING PROCESS MODEL

This model describes a process that can help you plan and prepare for any influencing challenge you face.

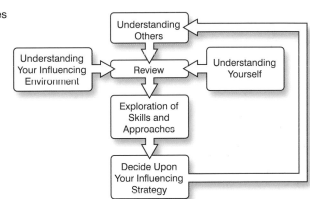

Adapted from Dent & Brent 2001

LEADERS AND INFLUENCE

THE INFLUENCING PROCESS MODEL

DESCRIPTION OF THE PROCESS

Understanding Others: analysing the stakeholders who are involved in your influencing issue, gathering as much information and intelligence as possible about the others.

Understanding Your Influencing Environment: being aware of the way things are done in the environment in which you are influencing. This is often referred to as understanding the culture of the organisation, division, department or whatever.

Understanding Yourself: your values and beliefs, your strengths and weaknesses, your likes and dislikes and your style when relating to others.

Review: at this stage you should review the information you have collected and consider how it can be used to assist you when planning and preparing to influence.

Exploration of Skills and Approaches: you can now begin to decide upon the influencing skills, approaches and tactics to employ in meeting your objective.
At this stage you might begin to reflect on the need to adopt different approaches for different people in different situations and to plan for this eventuality.

Decide upon Your Influencing Strategy: if you've followed all the above stages you will probably start to recognise that influencing is about *different strokes for different folks*.

INFLUENCING SKILLS AND QUALITIES

Influencing involves communicating with others in order to reach an effective outcome. You need to gain commitment to ideas and actions so that all parties feel they have had an opportunity to contribute and have bought into the outcome.

Communication skills are essential for successful influencing:

- Active listening
- Verbal fluency
- Questioning
- Probing
- Testing understanding
- Summarising
- Awareness of body language
- Visioning

In addition to these skills, all of which contribute to your presentation of your influencing issues, certain important qualities will contribute to effective outcomes:

- Self-confidence
- Flexibility
- Enthusiasm
- Patience
- Credibility
- Courage

LEADERS AND INFLUENCE

INFLUENCING TECHNIQUES/APPROACHES

The techniques and approaches you adopt when influencing are largely dependent upon the influencing environment, the others involved and your own preferences on style and approach. If you accept that influencing is a long-term process then you should also agree that influencing starts when you begin any level of dialogue with your stakeholders.

So, during the preparatory phase you will typically take part in discussions to:

- Network
- Research and test your ideas
- Test others' views
- Establish your credibility
- Plant ideas for nurturing later in the process

Following the preparatory phase you will begin to plan how best to influence each of the others involved. Typically, the approaches adopted are:

- One-to-one meetings
- Meetings either influencing within the group or influencing to the group
- Influential presentations
- A written report/e-mail

Most effective influencing involves verbal communication of some sort or another. However, written communication can also form part of the process, though it is rarely effective on its own.

LEADERS AND INFLUENCE

DEVELOPING YOUR INFLUENCING STRATEGY

Exercise: using the model suggested on the previous pages think of a recent influencing situation when you were **unsuccessful**. Describe the situation. What was it that made you unsuccessful?

_____

_____

_____

Now focus on a recent situation when you were **successful**. Describe it and what it was that made you successful.

_____

_____

_____

LEADERS AND INFLUENCE

DEVELOPING YOUR INFLUENCING STRATEGY

Your influencing strategy is a combination of the skills, knowledge, ability and process adopted when you enter into a situation that demands changes in behaviour/attitude by one or other of the parties involved.

The strategy adopted will vary depending upon the people involved (the stakeholders), your relationship with these people, the situation/environment that exists at the time and your own particular preferences and blend of skills and aptitudes.

The strategy will, however, usually involve:

- Preparation and planning
- Review of all the parties involved
- Preferences in terms of approach – one-to-one, meetings, big groups, verbal, written
- Understanding of the outcome desired

There is no one perfect influencing strategy, rather there are different approaches for different situations. By reflecting on the messages emerging from your own personal review of what works and what doesn't for you (the exercise on the previous page) you should begin to formulate your own personal influencing strategy.

LEADERS AND CHANGE

ADAPT OR STAGNATE

One of the toughest challenges facing any leader is dealing with change - not only your own attitude to change but, more importantly, effecting change in the people around you.

It is becoming a bit of a cliché to state it but change is a fact of life for all of us. Changes in society, organisations, technology, our markets, relationships, customers, etc mean that we must as individuals adapt or stagnate.

As a leader, learning to adapt is the only real answer. If you do not then you will undoubtedly stagnate and even die - metaphorically speaking, of course!

**Dinosaurs died out! Mammals did not!
Instead they embraced change and survived.**

LEADERS AND CHANGE

EXERCISE: CHANGES IN MY LIFE

Take a sheet of paper and draw a grid similar to this example.

CHANGE TIME	ACTUAL CHANGE	FEELINGS	PROCESS ADOPTED

My change philosophy

- Decide on your own timing, eg: changes in the last year, 5 years, 10 years or select stages in your life (0-20/20-30/30-40, etc)

- Identify the changes that have affected you: for instance, career change, parents separating, leaving school, moving house, going to university, changing jobs, redundancy, etc

- Identify the feelings you had at the time of the change

- How did you deal with the change? Note down the stages you went through in adapting to the change

- Now reflect on these four stages and note how you actually dealt with the change and how your approach has changed over the years - in other words, summarise your change philosophy

LEADERS AND CHANGE

HAVE YOU ADAPTED?

By raising your own awareness of how you react to and deal with change you may become more aware of how change can affect those around you.

Now think about your leadership responsibilities and the people you are responsible for - your followers!

- What changes have affected you and your followers in the last week/month/year/five years?

- What responses have you noticed, both your own and those of others?

- How have you dealt with these responses and adapted to the change?

The key question is, **have you adapted?**

A PROCESS FOR LEADING CHANGE

Awareness of need for change
- a feeling of discomfort with the current environment/situation
- a realisation that things can't continue as they are

Confirming the change
- share with others the benefits and rewards
- communicate to all the outcomes
- put processes in place to maintain and mirror the change

Creating a change mindset in others
- communicating and creating a sense of urgency
- gaining commitment and motivation
- recognising that anxieties exist

Providing support for the change
- involving everyone in the process
- celebrating and rewarding small changes
- providing skill development opportunities

Communicating the change message
- why the change is necessary
- linking the past with the future
- providing the parameters for change

AWARENESS OF THE NEED FOR CHANGE

Both you and your people must be aware of the need to change. Change is a painful process and people resist it mainly because of fear of the unknown. Your job is to let people know that to change is a necessity, not a *nice to have*, but **vital**.

In dealing with personal change, awareness often comes about from some sort of negative situation (for instance, loss of a job, illness, divorce, redundancy) which causes a degree of stress.

Creating this awareness in others demands that you the leader communicate why the change is necessary:

- Tell your people the truth
- Communicate the current situation
- Identify the implications of doing nothing
- Be brutally honest

Unless resistance can be overcome change will never take place.

CREATING A CHANGE MINDSET IN OTHERS

Raising awareness is the first step, but actually creating a mindset of change in others demands real guts from the leader.

Your first challenge is to get your key players or influencers on board. They can then assist you in the change process. It is vital that you spend time talking to them, sharing your own anxieties about the future and being completely honest about why change is necessary.

During this whole process you must be aware of the anxieties that exist. People will be fearful of the unknown:

- For their jobs
- For the future
- Changes in their routine, role and responsibilities

Getting commitment from others is a time-consuming process. It will demand patience and understanding on your part. Listening is probably your biggest ally at this stage of the change process. You must listen not only with your ears but also with your eyes, observing what's going on around you and being totally aware of how others are responding and acting.

LEADERS AND CHANGE

COMMUNICATING THE CHANGE MESSAGE

Communicating the change message to others means:

- Being absolutely clear about why change is necessary - sharing the truth about what has caused the change to take place, even if that means admitting your own failings

- Looking back at what has been successful in the past and how change has also been part of past success

- Looking forward to share your own vision of the future and to encourage others to contribute to that future and the vision

- Identifying and setting objectives, goals, boundaries for change - people need to know when changes are beginning to happen and what the consequences of them are

- Providing opportunities for people to review and reflect on the process to enable any changes to be confirmed

'Change is the law of life. And those who look only to the past or the present are certain to miss the future.'
John F Kennedy

PROVIDING SUPPORT FOR CHANGE

Change usually means that people have to learn new skills, new ways of working and how to deal with different situations.

As a leader you must provide opportunities for people to develop and try out new approaches. Your support role here should be to:

- Reward
- Celebrate
- Provide feedback
- Confirm new skills
- Provide the resources to develop
- Act as a coach or mentor
- Allow mistakes and learn from them

Above all recognise that people need time, space and the right atmosphere to really adapt to new circumstances and change.

CONFIRMING THE CHANGE

Inevitably, change will mean that new processes and practices are necessary as part of your day-to-day routine and/or organisational life.

It is important for the continuation of the change process and to confirm change as a new competence for all those involved that successes are celebrated and rewarded. You should:

- Publicise outcomes of the change, especially success stories
- Reward both individuals and the organisation for success
- Confirm new processes and practices as part of organisational life
- Ensure that everyone regards change as part of their everyday life and that it is exciting and rewarding to be part of it

LEADERS AND CHANGE

EXERCISE: CHANGE REVIEW

Think about a change you have recently experienced and review and reflect on the aspects of the change that you liked and disliked.

- Things I liked

- Things I disliked

_____   _____

_____   _____

_____   _____

_____   _____

_____   _____

Now examine the two lists. What does this tell you about your approach to change and what steps might you now take to lengthen the *liked* list?

'Leadership produces change. That is its primary function.'
John Kotter

LEADERS AND SOCIAL RESPONSIBILITY

LEADERS AND SOCIAL RESPONSIBILITY

CHANGING CONTEXT FOR LEADERS

The ideas that define business leadership constantly evolve in response to societal, political, economic and cultural changes. These long-term changes and trends are beginning to have a significant impact on how leaders are operating in business today. A new generation is emerging, of leaders who increasingly recognise the need for responsible leadership and management practices that take account both of the changing societal context and our increasing concerns about sustainability and climate change.

LEADERS AND SOCIAL RESPONSIBILITY

'In today's world
I don't think you have a choice.
If you are going to be an effective leader
you've really got to be driving all aspects of
sustainability as part of what you are doing,
because it's the right thing to do and because
it's the right thing to do for the business.'

John Brock,
Coca Cola Enterprises

LEADERS AND SOCIAL RESPONSIBILITY

NEW PERSPECTIVE

Successful organisations and their leaders in this new world will have to:

- Understand why corporate social responsibility is important for their organisation
- Define the important issues for their industry/organisation
- Secure the commitment and buy-in of all management levels
- Set goals, priorities and policies as part of the existing management processes
- Educate staff about this new way of thinking and behaving
- Set targets, develop action plans and dedicate resources to achievement in this area
- Make it visible to all – in many organisations today, for instance, we see recycling bins in all offices. This is often supported by reporting about the percentage recycling the organisation has achieved over particular time scales: a small yet visible symbol

LEADERS AND SOCIAL RESPONSIBILITY

THE EVOLVING LEADERSHIP ROLE

Contemporary business leaders must be aware of the major forces shaping society today and understand how their organisations need to respond and contribute to these challenges. It is their role to lead and drive change to create value for their organisation and society in general.

A different perspective on the business leader's role and purpose

Leading change across the business

Leading change beyond business boundaries

Adapted from *Leading in a Rapidly Changing World: How business leaders are reframing success* – A United Nations report by Ashridge and the International Business Leaders Forum, March 2012

LEADERS AND SOCIAL RESPONSIBILITY

THE EVOLVING LEADERSHIP ROLE

Leader's role and purpose – a different perspective

- Business works in partnership with political leaders, civil leaders and other stakeholders
- Business leaders address societal challenges as part of their core business
- Business leaders must understand the major forces shaping society
- Business leaders need to respond in a way that benefits their business and the wider community

Leading change across the business

- Make links between external trends and the core business
- Encourage innovation
- Use language and symbols effectively
- Influence mindsets and culture
- Create appropriate metrics
- Recognise and reward new behaviour
- Provide support when needed
- Have the courage of your convictions

Leading change beyond business boundaries

- Contribute to public debate and share your point of view and experience
- Lead the way in your industry and profession
- Engage with others to broaden and deepen both your own and others' perspectives
- Collaborate with others to drive change in the wider community and world.

  Adapted from *Leading in a Rapidly Changing World: How business leaders are reframing success*, A United Nations report by Ashridge and the International Business Leaders Forum, March 2012

LEADERS AND SOCIAL RESPONSIBILITY

'The people we get have a rare combination of being as committed to altruism as they are to commercialism; they want to win financially and environmentally. When you get the two together it's really powerful.'

Richard Reed,
Founder, Innocent Drinks

FINAL THOUGHTS

TEN TIPS FOR EFFECTIVE LEADERS

- Know your own strengths and weaknesses - be self-aware
- Know your leadership network
- Get to know your people and what makes them tick
- Surround yourself with great people
- Get a coach
- Prepare the way - this is vital
- Maintain a positive mental attitude
- Have faith in yourself
- Be your own person
- Create and develop your own authentic brand of leadership

FINAL THOUGHTS

LEADERSHIP MNEMONIC

Here's my personal leadership mnemonic. Create your own mnemonic:

L	– Luck	L _____
E	– Enthusiasm	E _____
A	– Authenticity	A _____
D	– Drive	D _____
E	– Energy	E _____
R	– Respect	R _____
S	– Sensitivity	S _____
H	– Humour	H _____
I	– Integrity	I _____
P	– Passion	P _____

READING LIST

ESSENTIAL READING ABOUT LEADERSHIP

Primal Leadership: Unleashing the Power of Emotional Intelligence
by Professor D. Goleman, R. Boyatzis & A. McKee, HBR 2013

The Leaders Guide to Managing People: How to use soft skills to get hard results
by M. Brent & F. E. Dent, Pearsons 2014

JP Kotter on What Leaders Really Do
by John P Kotter: HBR 1999

HBR's 10 Must Reads on Leadership
by Harvard Business Review 2011

Develop Your Leadership Skills
by John Adair: Kogan Page 2010

Leadership And The One Minute Manager
by Drea Zigarmi, Kenneth Blanchard & Patricia Zigarmi: Harper Collins 2000

Relax, It's Only Uncertainty: Lead The Way When The Way Is Changing
by Phillip Hodgson, Randall P White: FT Prentice Hall 2001

The Leadership Mystique: A User's Manual For The Human Enterprise
by F R Manfred Kets de Vries: Pearson Education Limited 2001

Why Should Anyone Be Led By YOU? What It Takes To Be An Authentic Leader
by Rob Goffee and Gareth Jones: Harvard Business School Press 2006

READING LIST

ESSENTIAL READING ABOUT LEADERS

Jack: What I've Learned Leading A Great Company and Great People
by Jack Welch: Headline 2001

21 Leaders For The 21st Century - How Innovative Leaders Manage In The Digital Age
by Fons Trompenaars & Charles Hampden Turner: Capstone 2001

Steve Jobs
by Walter Isaacson: Little, Brown 2011

John F Kennedy, Commander-in-Chief: A Profile In Leadership
by Pierre Salinger: Penguin 1997

Losing My Virginity: An Autobiography
by Richard Branson: Virgin Books 2002

The Illustrated Walk To Freedom
by Nelson Mandela: Little, Brown 2001

The World According To Margaret Thatcher
by Margaret Thatcher: Michael O Mara 2003

Living Leadership: A Practical Guide For Ordinary Heroes
by George Binney, Gerhard Wilke & Colin Williams: FT Prentice Hall 2005

Inside Coca Cola
by Neville Isdell: St Martins Press 2012

About the Author

Fiona Elsa Dent, MA, MSc, Chartered FCIPD, FHEA
Fiona is an independent management trainer, consultant, coach and author. She spent over 20 years on the faculty at Ashridge Business School and continues to work with them as a leadership coach and tutor on various programmes. She is predominantly interested in helping people to develop their personal skills to be the best they can be. Her particular specialisms are influencing, interpersonal and relationship skills.

Her books cover topics such as influencing, people management skills, self-managed development, women in business and coaching and mentoring. She has written two other Pocketbooks: *'Working Relationships'* and *'Self-managed Development'*; her latest publications are *'The Leader's Guide to Coaching and Mentoring: How to Use Soft Skills to get Hard Results'* (with Mike Brent, 2015) and *'How to Thrive and Survive as a Working Woman: The Coach Yourself Toolkit'* (with Viki Holton, 2016).

Contact

Fiona runs her own consultancy - FED Development Ltd and can be contacted on:
Email: FionaEDentbiz@gmail.com
Web: www.feddevelopment.co.uk
Mobile: 07976 370627

ORDER FORM

Your details

Name _____

Position _____

Company _____

Address _____

_____

_____

Telephone _____

Fax _____

E-mail _____

VAT No. (EC companies) _____

Your Order Ref _____

Please send me:

No. copies

The Leadership _____ Pocketbook [ ]

The _____ Pocketbook [ ]

The _____ Pocketbook [ ]

The _____ Pocketbook [ ]

Order by Post

MANAGEMENT POCKETBOOKS LTD
LAUREL HOUSE, STATION APPROACH,
ALRESFORD, HAMPSHIRE SO24 9JH UK

Order by Phone, Fax or Internet
Telephone: +44 (0)1962 735573
Facsimile: +44 (0)1962 733637
Email: sales@pocketbook.co.uk
Web: www.pocketbook.co.uk

Customers in USA should contact:
Management Pocketbooks
2427 Bond Street, University Park, IL 60466
Telephone: 866 620 6944 Facsimile: 708 534 7803
Email: mp.orders@ware-pak.com
Web: www.managementpocketbooks.com

Pocketbooks – *available in both paperback and digital formats*

360 Degree Feedback*
Absence Management
Appraisals
Assertiveness
Balance Sheet
Body Language
Business Planning
Career Transition
Coaching
Cognitive Behavioural Coaching
Communicator's
Competencies
Confidence
Creative Manager's
C.R.M.
Cross-cultural Business
Customer Service
Decision-making
Delegation
Developing People
Discipline & Grievance
Diversity*
Emotional Intelligence
Empowerment*
Energy and Well-being
Engagement
Facilitator's
Feedback
Flexible Working

Handling Complaints
Handling Resistance
Icebreakers
Impact & Presence
Improving Efficiency
Improving Profitability
Induction*
Influencing
Interviewer's
I.T. Trainer's
Key Account Manager's
Leadership
Learner's
Learning Needs Analysis
Management Models
Manager's
Managing Assessment Centres
Managing Budgets
Managing Cashflow
Managing Change
Managing Customer Service
Managing Difficult Participants
Managing Recruitment
Managing Upwards
Managing Your Appraisal
Marketing
Mediation
Meetings
Memory

Mentoring
Mindfulness at Work
Motivation
Negotiator's
Networking
NLP
Nurturing Innovation
Openers & Closers
People Manager's
Performance Management
Personal Success
Positive Mental Attitude
Presentations
Problem Behaviour
Project Management
Psychometric Testing
Resolving Conflict
Reward*
Sales Excellence
Salesperson's*
Self-managed Development
Starting In Management
Storytelling
Strategy
Stress
Succeeding at Interviews
Sustainability
Tackling Difficult Conversations
Talent Management

Teambuilding Activities
Teamworking
Telephone Skills
Thinker's
Time Management
Trainer's
Training Evaluation
Transfer of Learning
Transformative Change
Virtual Teams
Vocal Skills
Webinars
Working Relationships
Workplace Politics
Writing Skills

* only available as an e-book

Pocketfiles

Trainer's Blue Pocketfile of
Ready-to-use Activities

Trainer's Green Pocketfile of
Ready-to-use Activities

Trainer's Red Pocketfile of
Ready-to-use Activities

To order please visit us at **www.pocketbook.co.uk**

18.05.16